FOREWORD TO THE TEACHER

Poor readers are unhappy pianists! These papers are designed to make reading easy and to increase the playing enjoyment of young pianists.

The **ABC PAPERS** are based on the idea that to see a note in relation to its preceding note is the first step toward fluency in reading ; to see and play a note in relation to its preceding note is what later becomes continuity or flow in music.

To see the following melody :

and recognize that the first note is C, play it , the next note is E, play it, the next note is C, play it, etc., is merely to read and play each of eight notes. But to see and play the first note, C, and then to see and play up a third, down a third, down a fourth, up a fourth, etc., is to see and feel a musical phrase.

The aim of these papers is to train students to recognize and play music from the standpoint of interval relationship rather than from the standpoint of individual notes.

This involves the following steps:
1. Recognizing intervals rapidly.
2. Playing intervals from dictation rapidly.
3. Recognizing and playing intervals simultaneously.

To facilitate these three steps, the teacher should give, in conjunction with the Papers, intensive drill on :
1. Developing the "feel" and "size" of intervals.
2. Playing without looking at the keyboard.
3. Ear - training and transposition.
4. Dictation :
   a. Teacher dictate -- student play.
   b. Teacher dictate -- student do mentally away from the keyboard.
   c. Teacher dictate -- student write on music paper.

Summy-Birchard Inc.
Exclusively distributed by Alfred Publishing Co., Inc.

Frances Clark

Draw a circle around each note that is on a line.

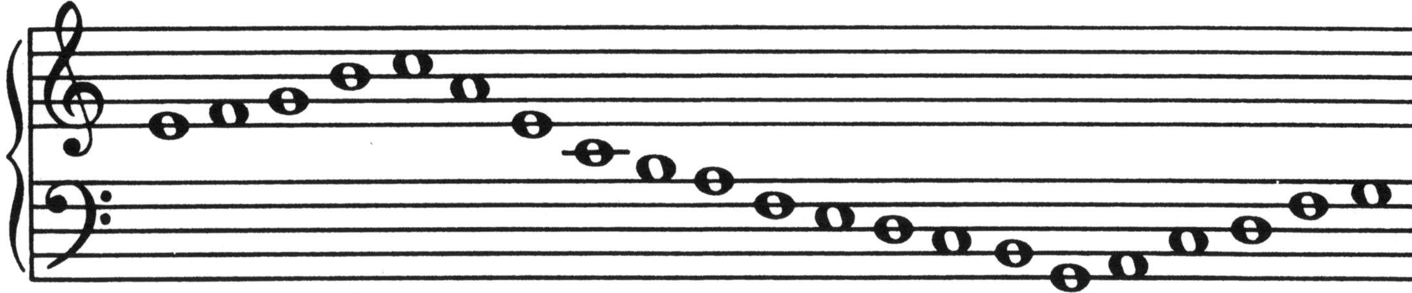

Draw a note on each line.

Draw a circle around each note that is in a space.

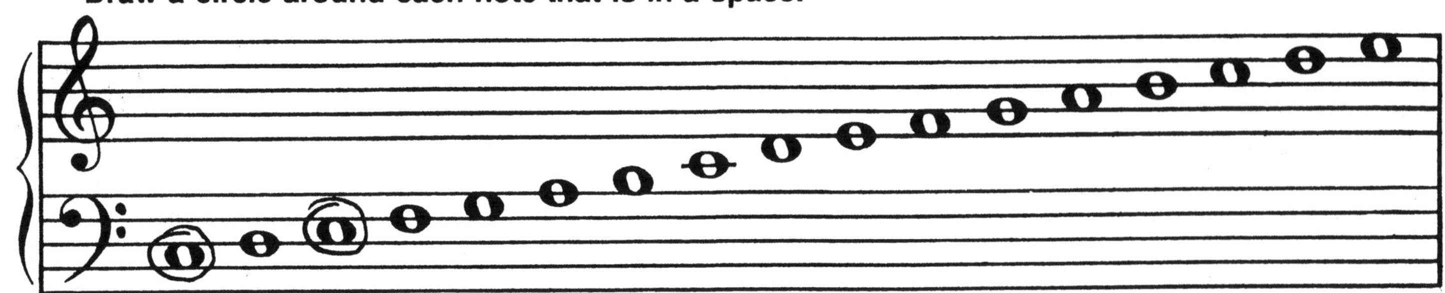

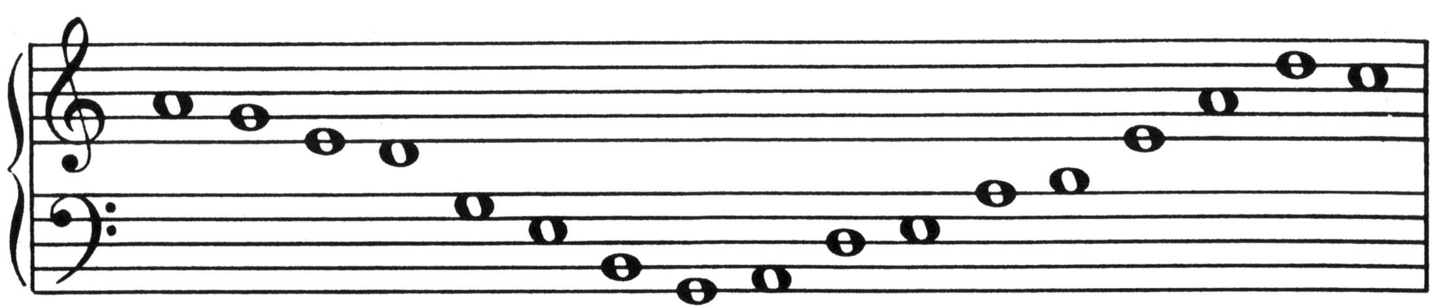

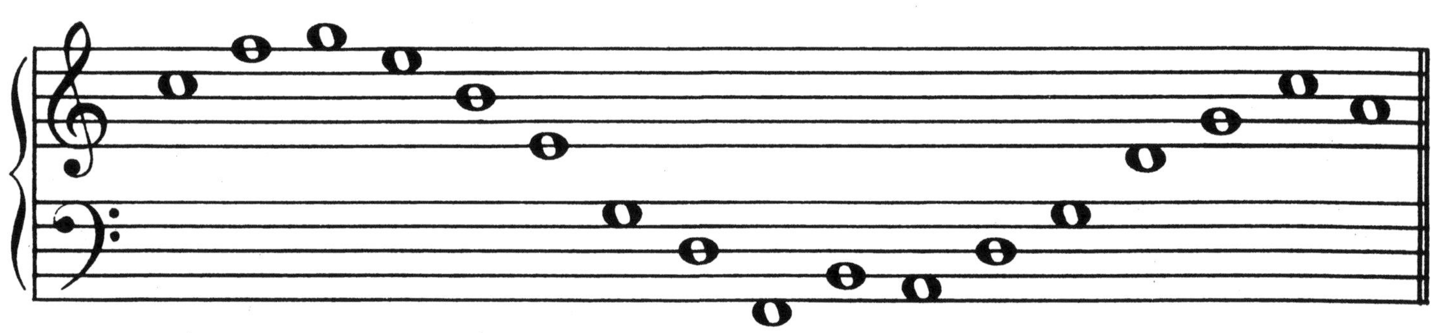

Draw a note in each space.

From one line to its nearest space is an interval of a second.
From one space to its nearest line is an interval of a second.

This is an exercise to learn the "Feel" of seconds.
Place your thumbs on middle C.

Now play it on the C above middle C and the C below middle C.

Draw lines showing whether the seconds go up or down.
Under each note write its name.

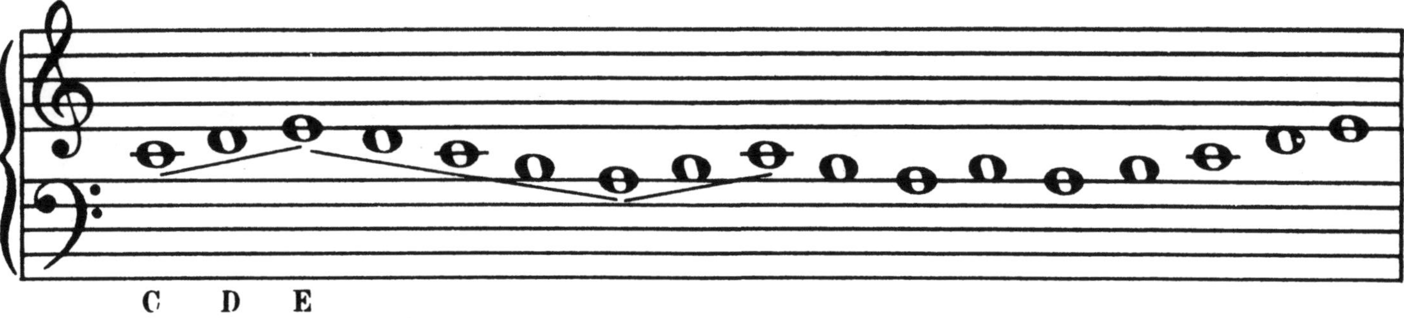

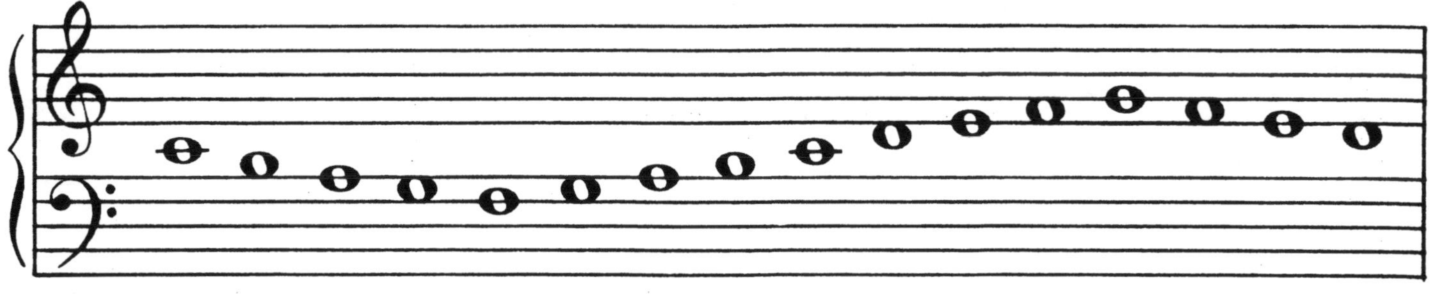

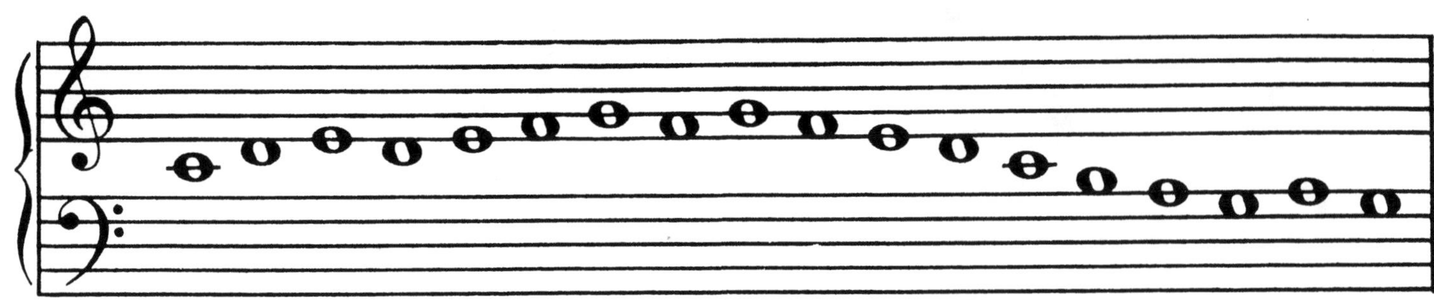

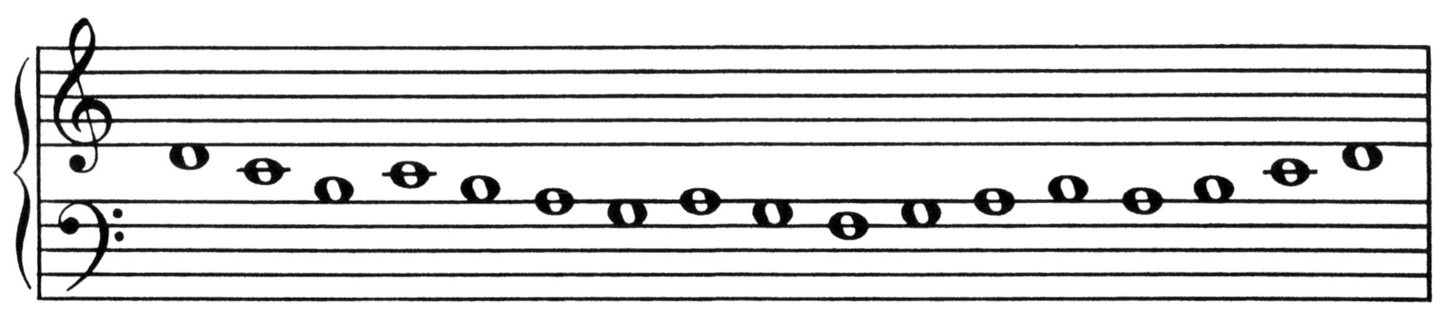

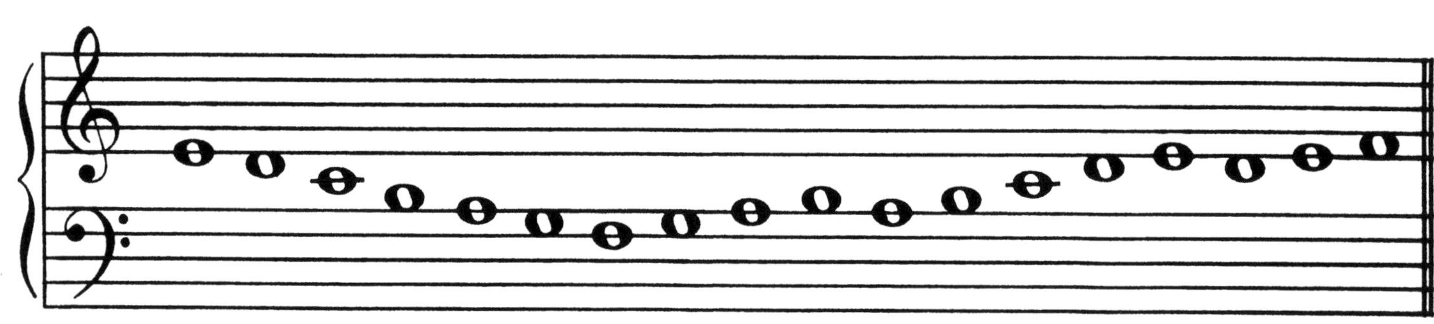

Learning to play without looking at the keyboard.

This is a picture of the keyboard:

You will see that the black keys are in groups of two's and three's. Without looking at the keyboard:

1. Place the fingers of your right hand around the group of two black keys in the middle of the piano.
2. "Pinch" them gently.
3. Without looking, slide your fingers up the keyboard to the group of three black keys.
4. "Pinch" them gently.

Go on sliding up the keyboard, pinching the groups of two black keys and three black keys, until you reach the top.

Then put the fingers of your left hand around the two black keys in the middle of the piano and go *down* the keyboard pinching the groups of two black keys and three black keys. *DO NOT LOOK AT THE KEYBOARD.*

Can you find all the groups of two black keys without looking at the keyboard?

The *white* key just below the *two* black keys is C.

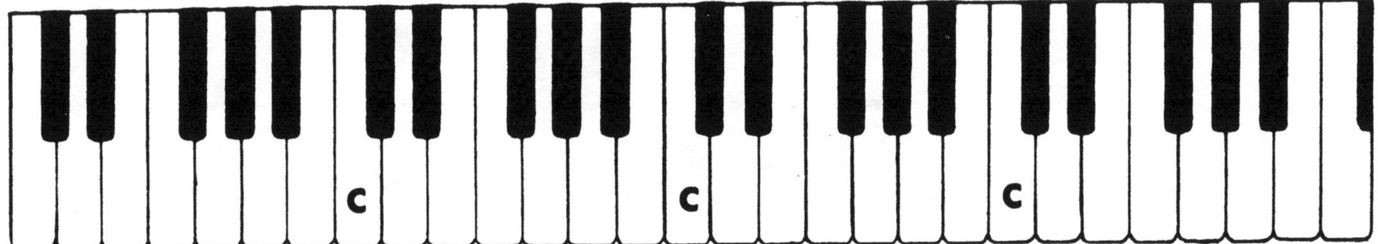

Without looking at the keyboard, find the group of two black keys in the middle of the piano – play middle C. You can find all the C's on the piano in this way.

The white key just *above* the two black key group is E. Play all E's on the piano.

Can you find all the three black key groups? The key just *below* the three black keys is F. The key *above* the three black keys is B.

Play all the F's on the piano.

Play all the B's on the piano.

Now you see how easy it is to find and play any note you wish, looking away from the keyboard!

Here are some pieces on seconds for you to play without looking at the keyboard.

For further practice in playing without looking at the keyboard.
1. Play these pieces on other C's.
2. Play No. 1 and No. 4 beginning on G.
3. Play Nos. 1, 2, 3 and 5 beginning on F.

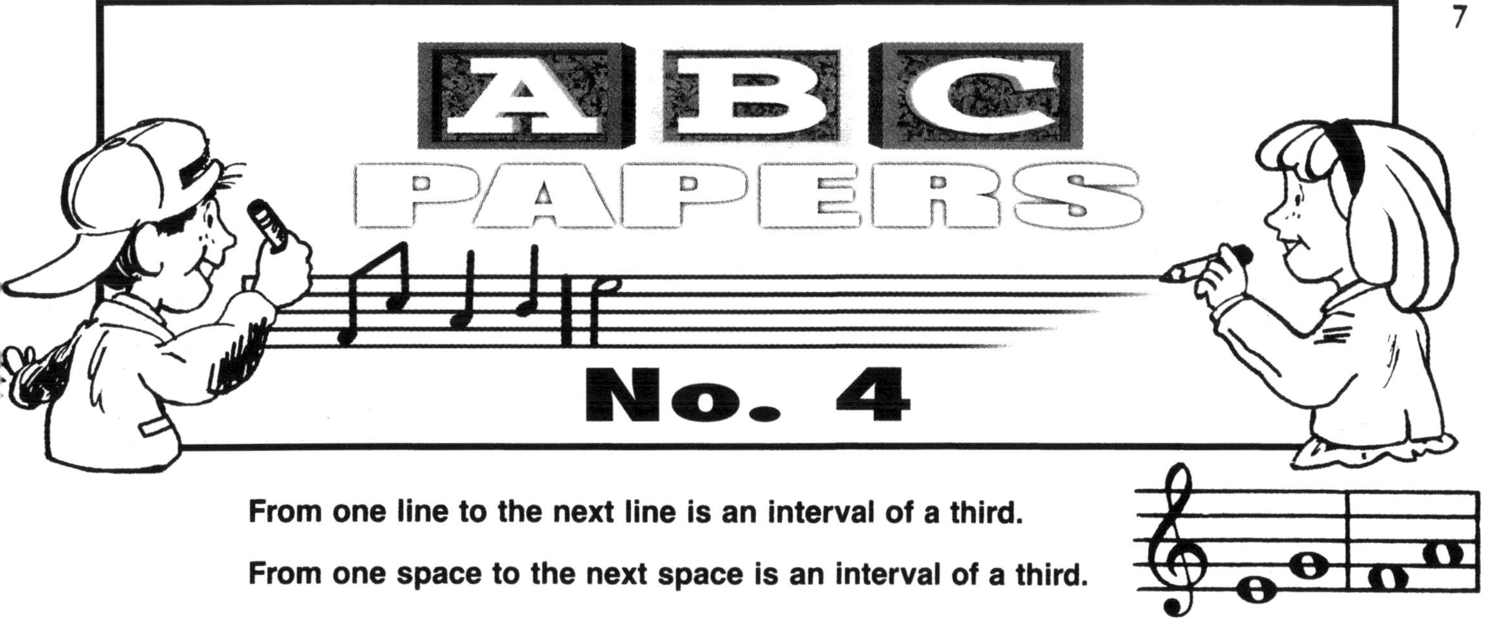

From one line to the next line is an interval of a third.

From one space to the next space is an interval of a third.

This is an exercise to learn the "Feel" of thirds.
Place your thumbs on middle C and play.

Now play it on the C above middle C and the C below middle C.
DON'T LOOK AT THE KEYBOARD!
Can you begin with your thumbs on F and play this same piece?
Can you play it on G? This is called transposing.

Indicate all intervals of a third.
Point and recite. i.e.: "C, down a second, down a second, down a third, up a second," etc.
Play and recite.

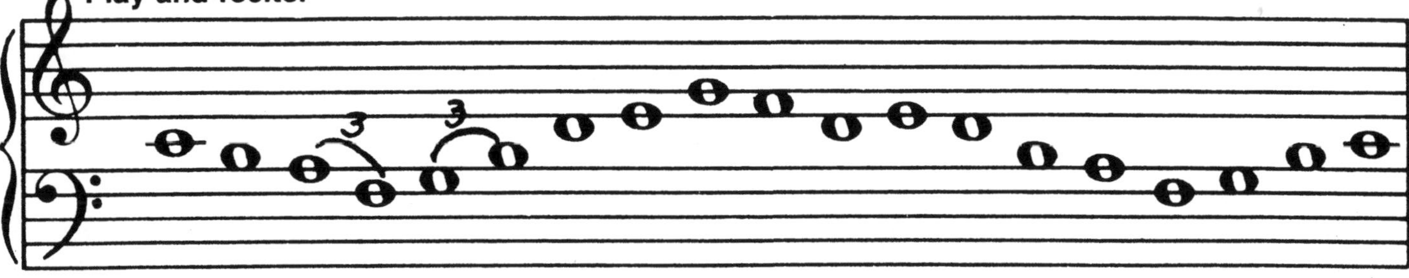

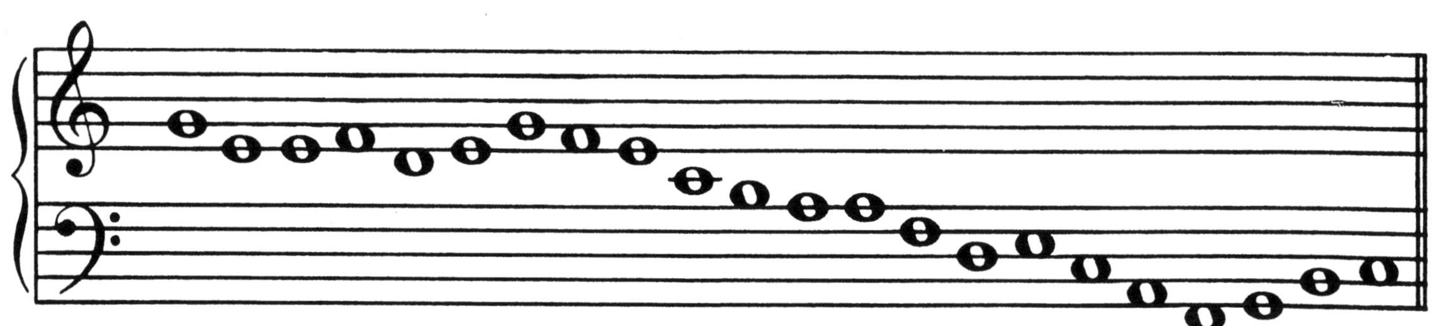

Now go back to the beginning and write the name under each of these notes.

Write the note a third above each of these notes.

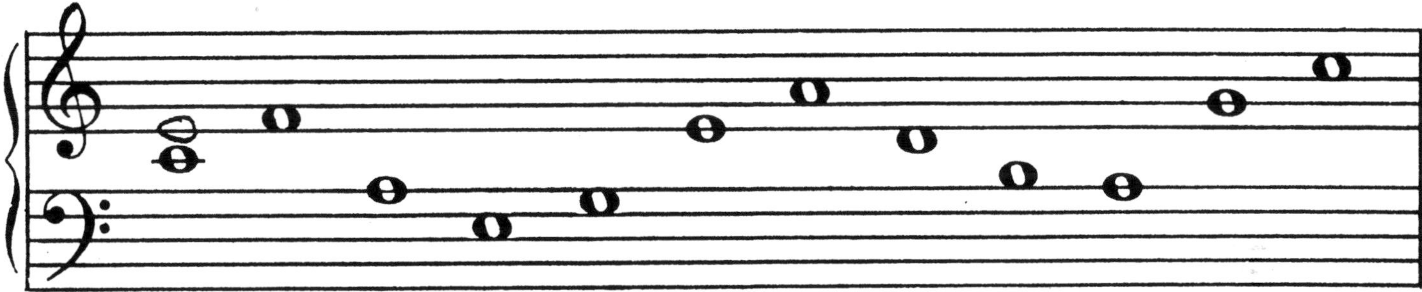

Write the note a third below each of these notes.

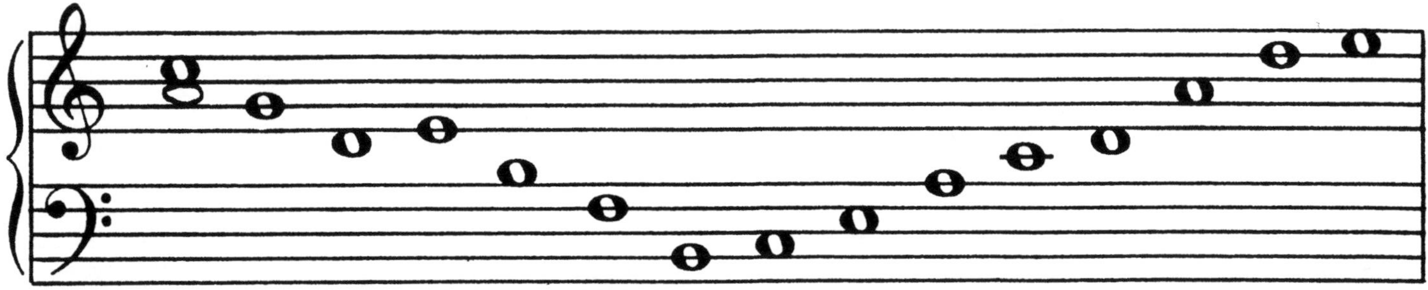

Dictation exercise:
Put the answer to each problem in its ☐

Example:

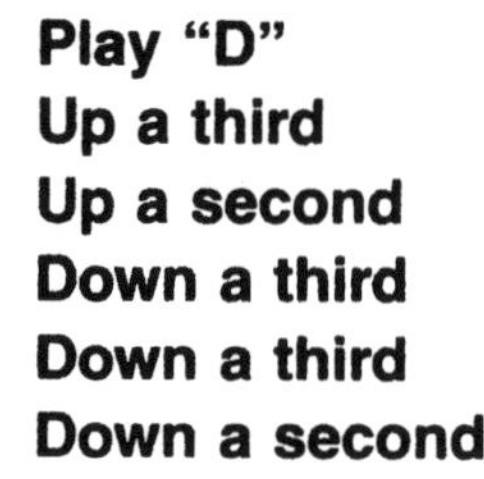

Play "D"
Up a third
Up a second
Down a third
Down a third
Down a second

B

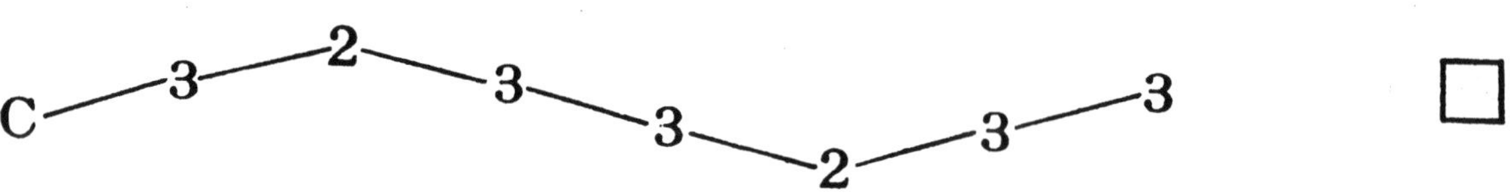

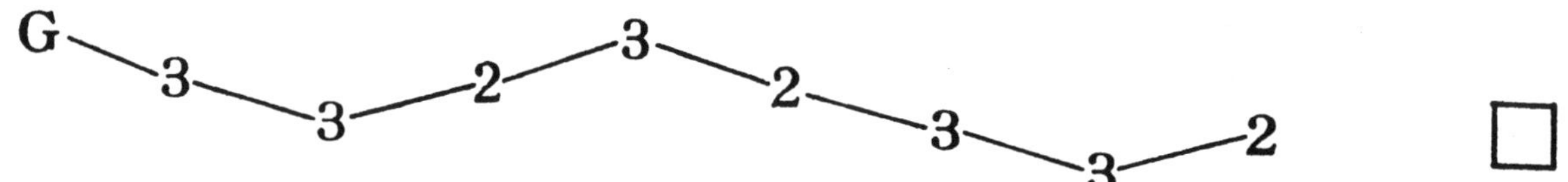

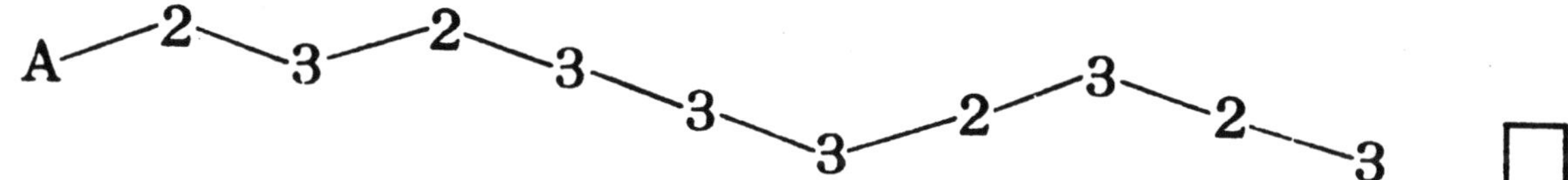

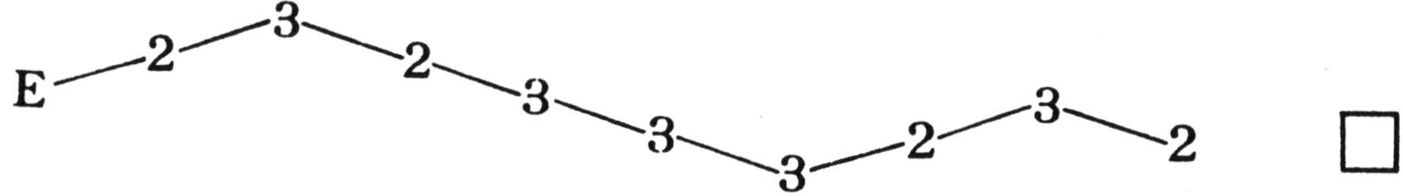

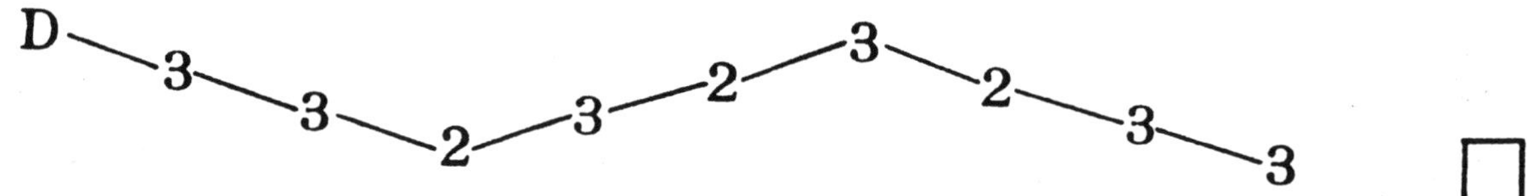

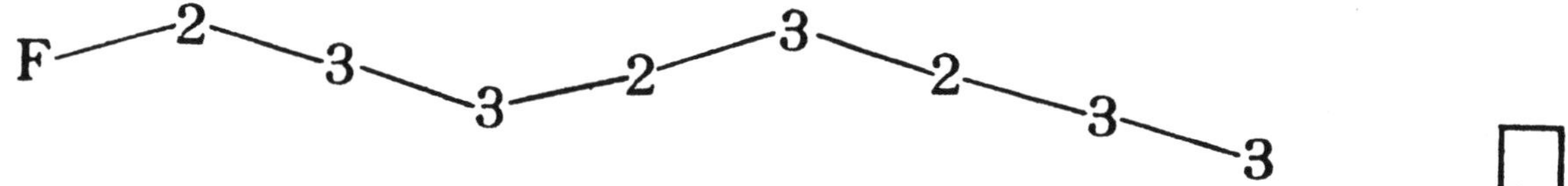

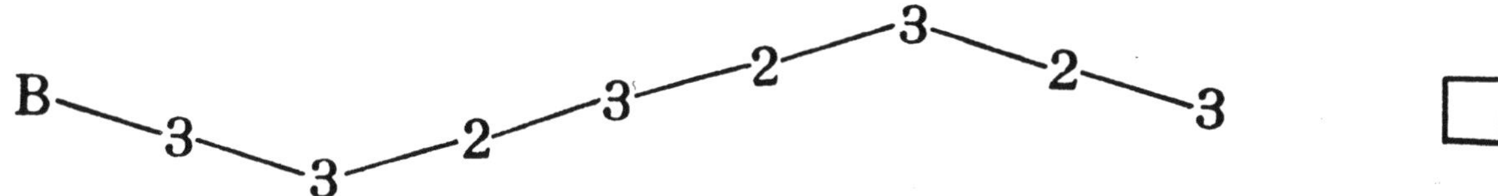

Divide these notes into measures.

Complete each measure with ONE note. Use ONE Note. Not more than ONE note!

Here are some pieces for you to play!
Watch for all intervals of a third. *REMEMBER NOT TO LOOK AT THE KEYBOARD.*

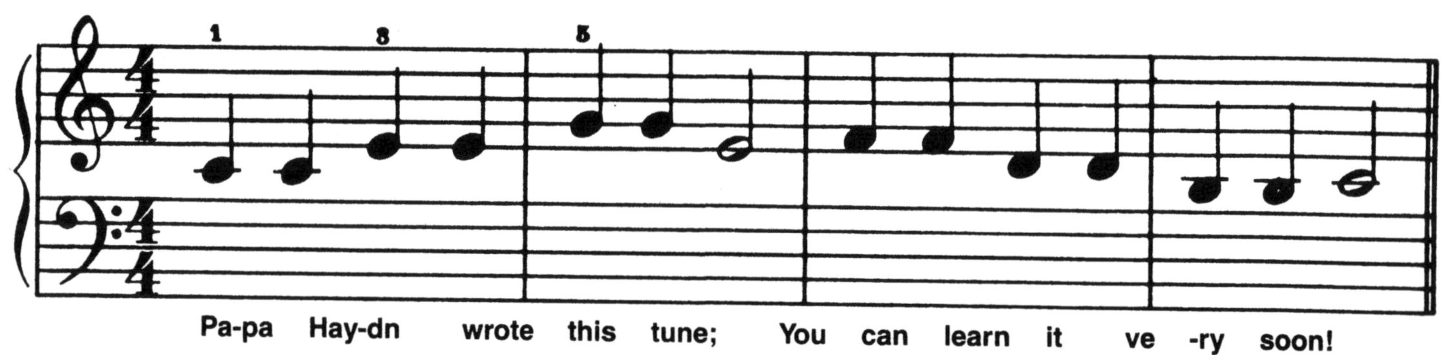

Your teacher will ask you to transpose these pieces.
Just remember the thirds and it will be easy.

Draw the note of a third *above* each of these notes.
Then draw the note a third *below* each of these notes.

Look at the notes you just drew. They are called triads.

Triads look like this  **Or like this** 

Write a triad on each of these notes.

A fifth is the top and bottom notes of a triad:

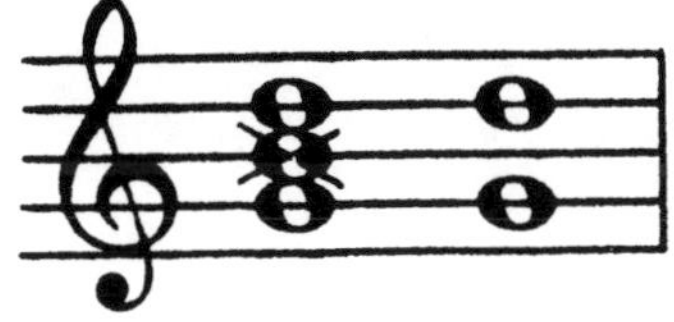 **Or** 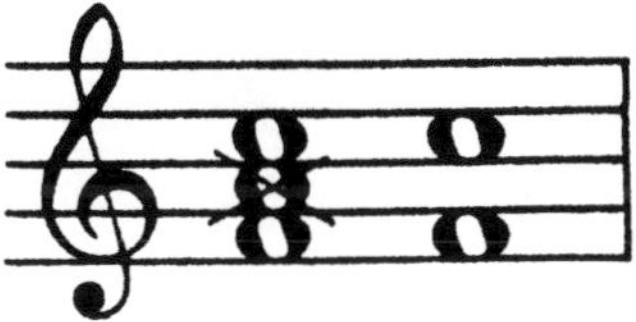

Thus, an interval of a fifth is on:

Two lines, with
one line between  **Or two spaces, with**
one space between 

This is an exercise to learn the "Feel" of fifths.
Play it on several C's, Then transpose it to other keys.
Don't look at the keyboard!

Indicate all intervals of a fifth.
Point and recite. i.e.: "C, down a fifth, down a fifth, up a second, up a fifth", etc.
Play and recite.

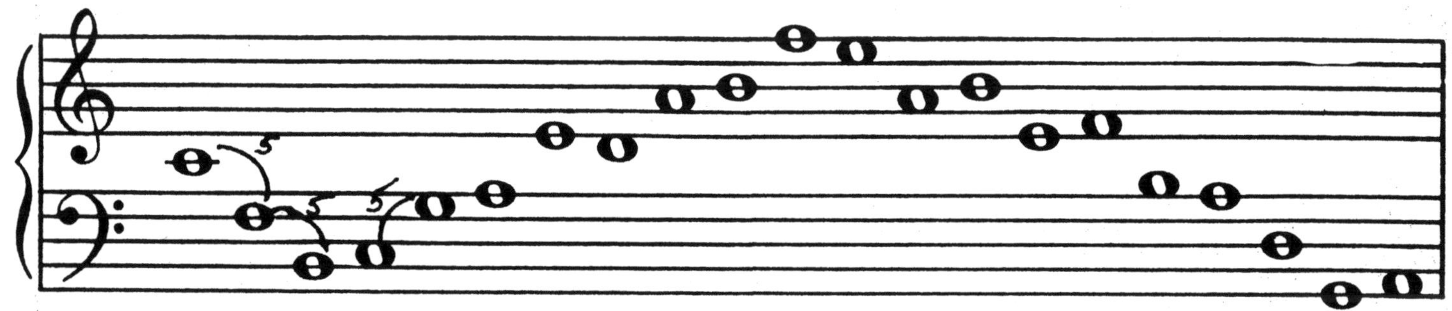

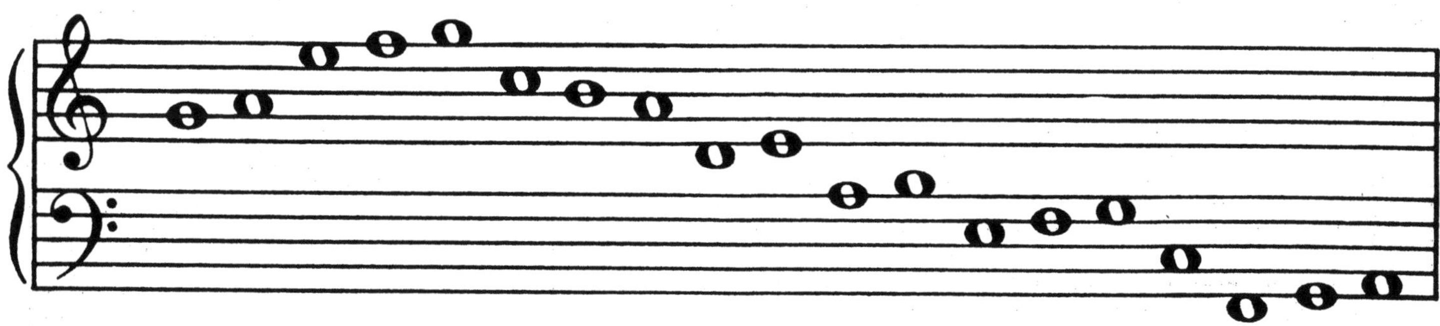

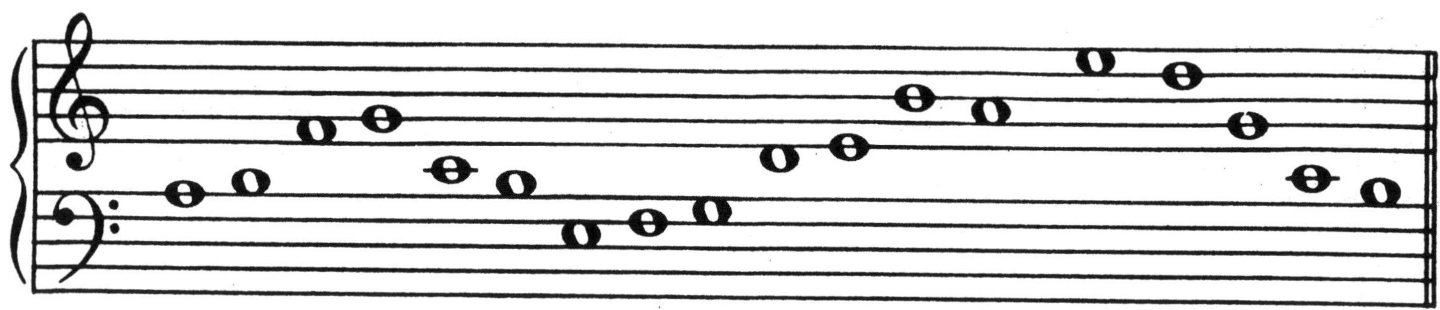

Write the name under each of these notes.

ABC PAPERS — No. 8

Indicate all intervals of thirds and fifths.*
Point and recite.
Play and recite.

*Because seconds pose no problem other than that of direction, and are so easily read as consecutive notes which move either up or down, the step of indicating seconds has been omitted throughout.

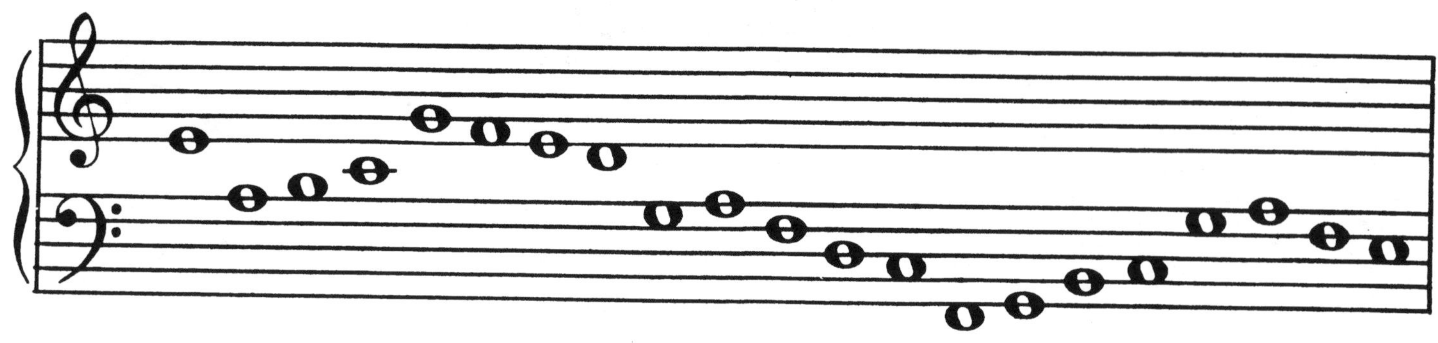

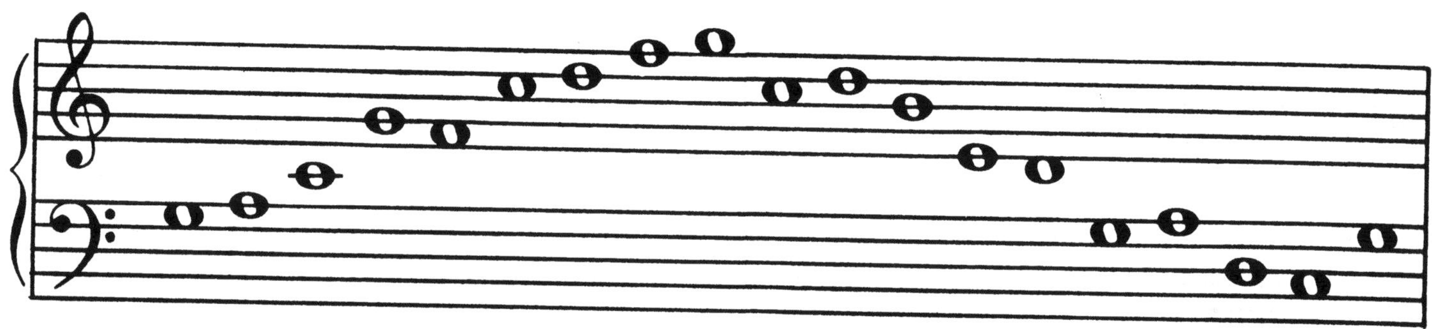

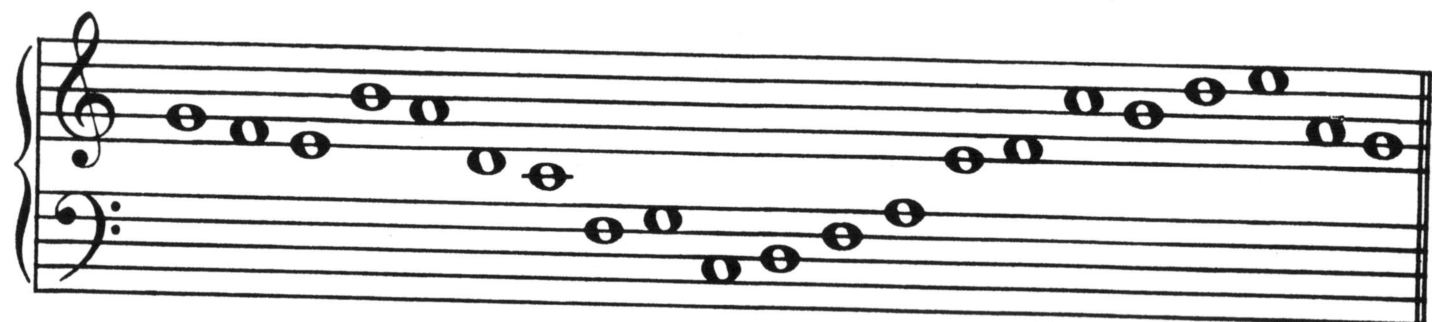

Now go back to the beginning and write the name under each of these notes.

Indicate all intervals of thirds and fifths.
Point and recite.
Play and recite.

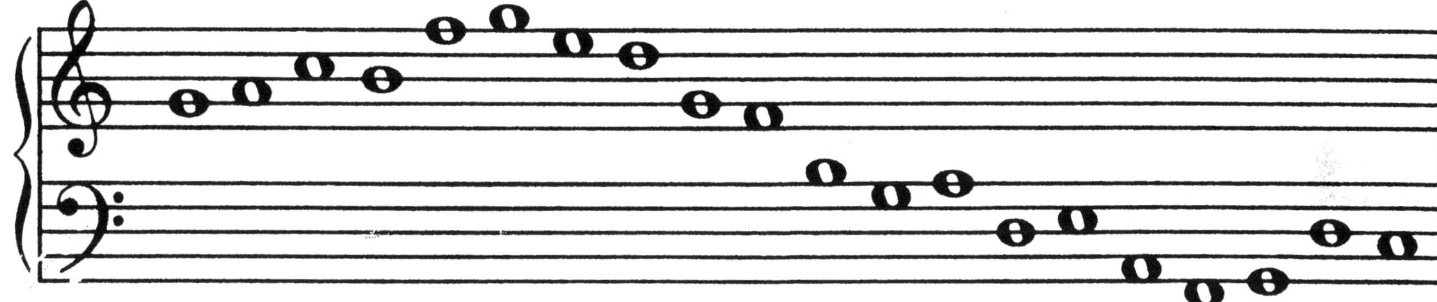

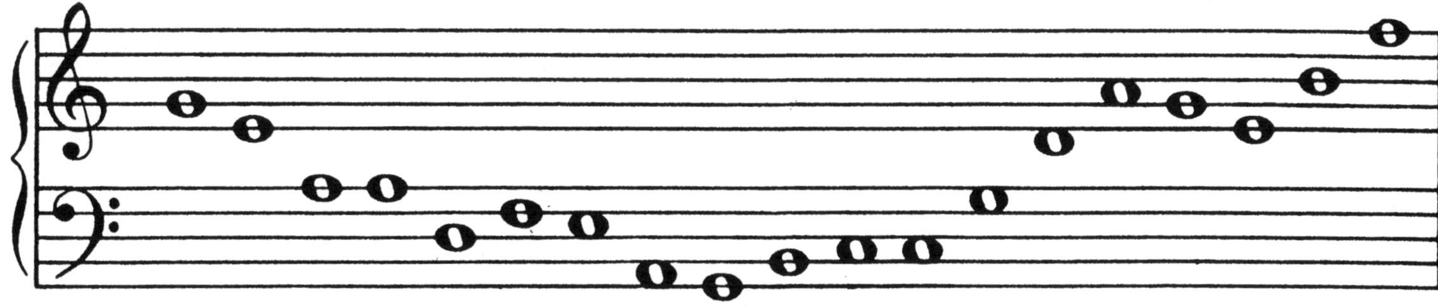

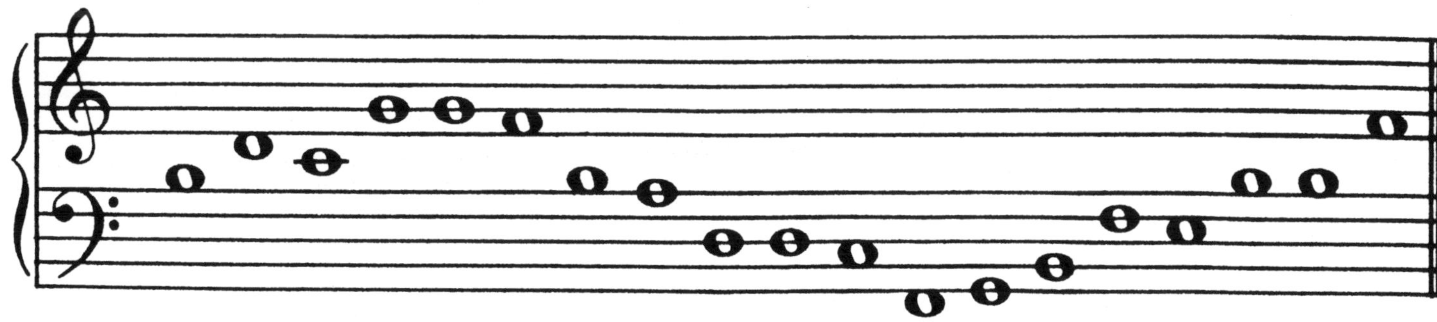

Dictation exercise:

Put the answer to each problem in its □

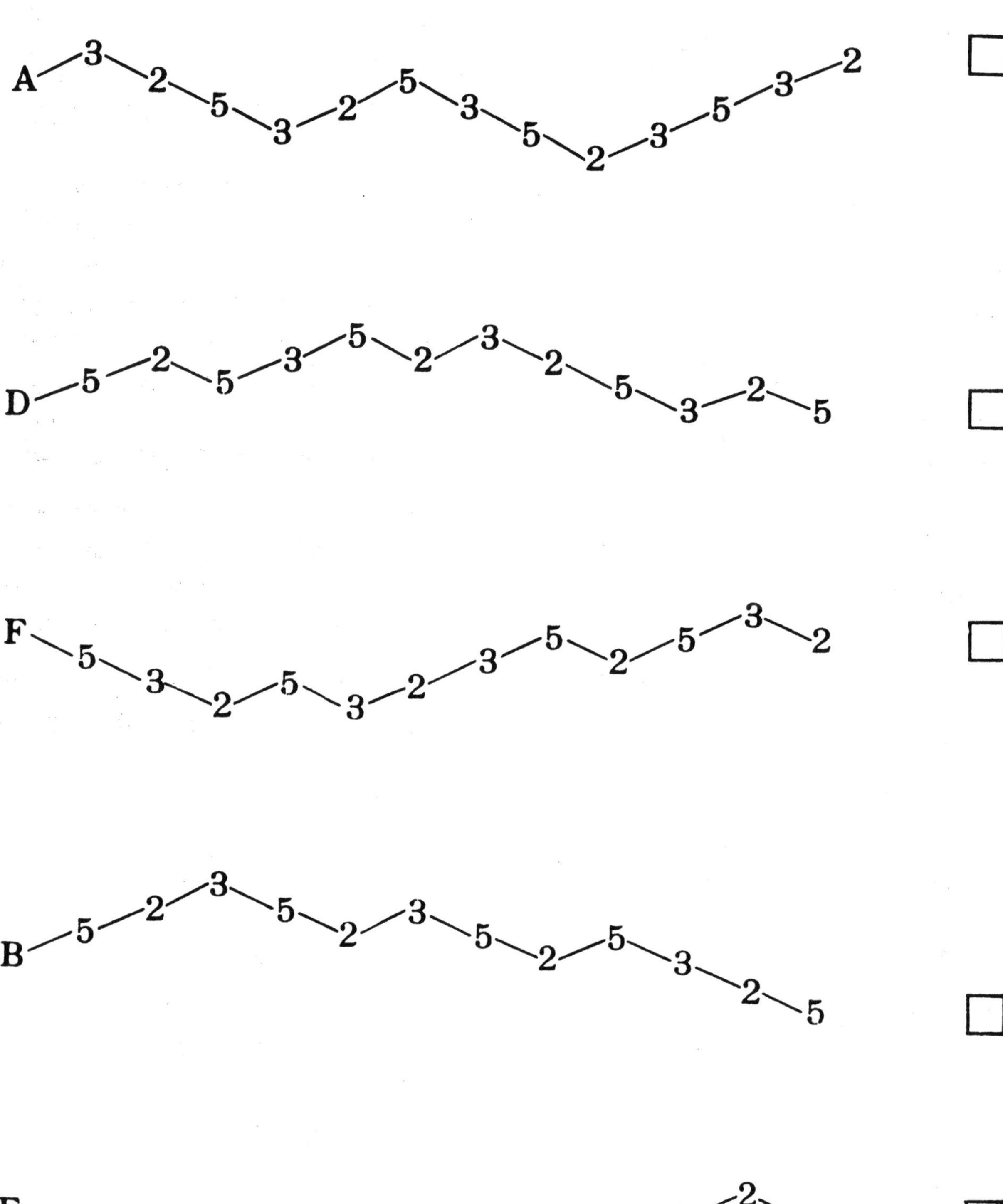

Divide these notes into measures.

Complete each measure with *ONE* note; use not more than *ONE* note!

Swing and count each measure

Here are some pieces for you to play. Can you find the thirds and fifths?

Put a check in the box if you played these without looking at the keyboard ☐
Transpose to other keys.

ABC PAPERS

No. 11

The notes of a *THIRD* are on two consecutive lines:

or on two con-secutive spaces:

The notes of a *FOURTH* are on a line and a space, with one line between:

or

This is an exercise to learn the "Feel" of fourths.
Play it on several C's and then transpose it to other keys.
DON'T LOOK AT THE KEYBOARD!

Indicate all intervals of a fourth.
Point and recite.
Play and recite.

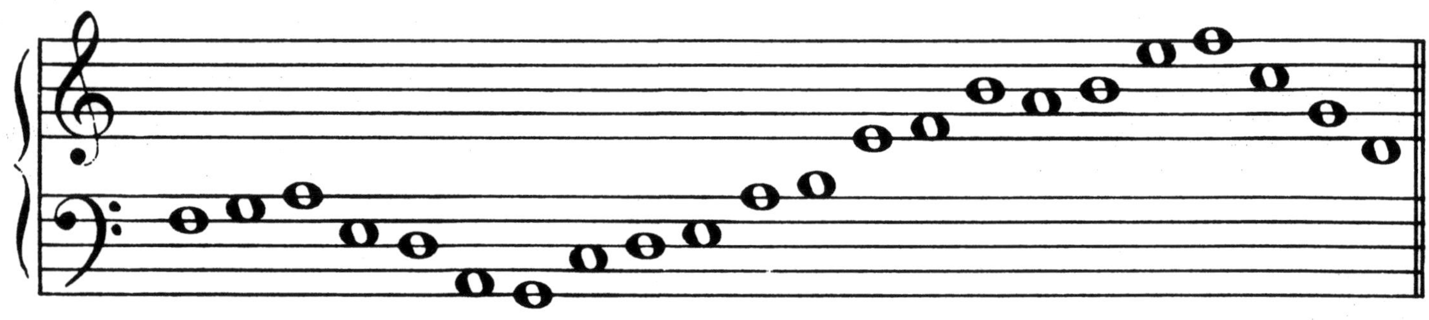

Go back to the beginning and write the name under each of these notes.

Draw the note a fourth above each of these notes.
Draw the note a fourth below each of these notes.

ABC
PAPERS
No. 12
Indicate all intervals of thirds, fourths, and fifths.
Point and recite.
Play and recite.

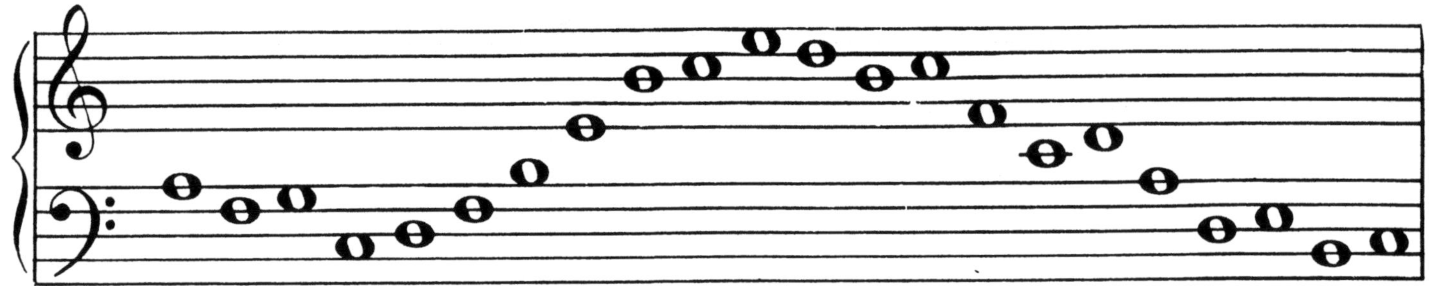

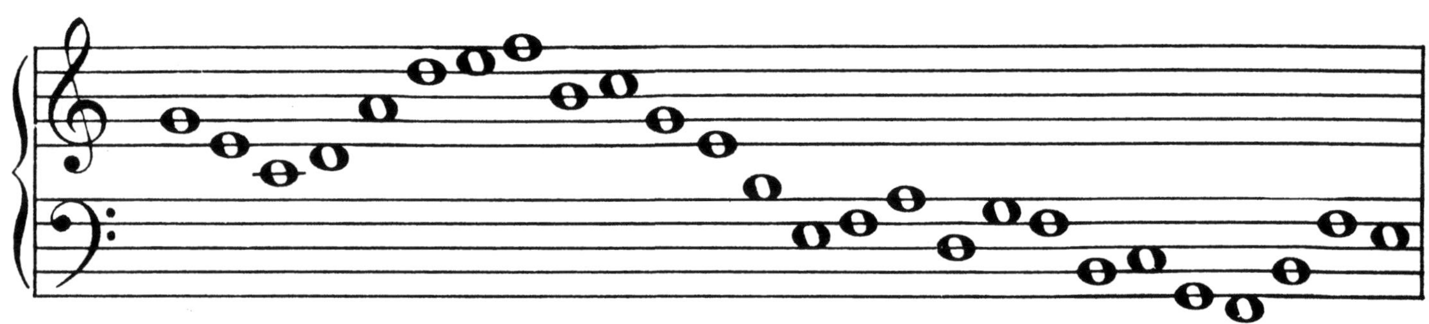

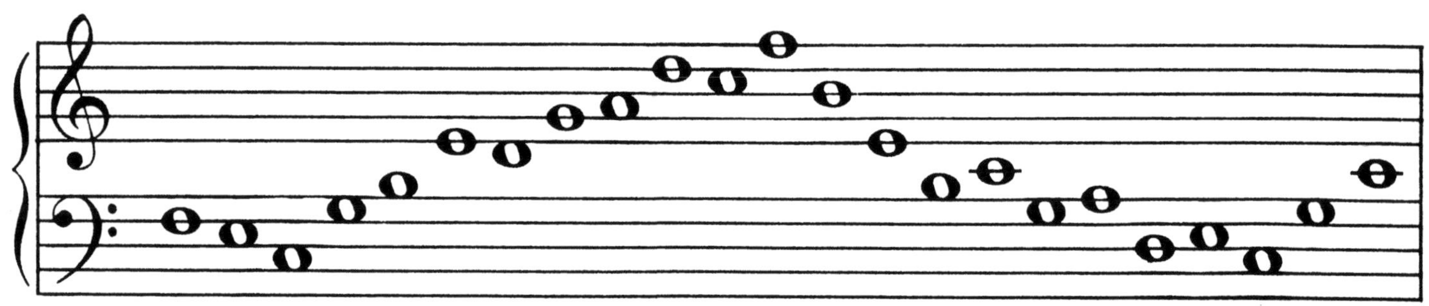

Now go back to the beginning and write the name under each of these notes.

What kind of intervals are these?
Put the number under each.

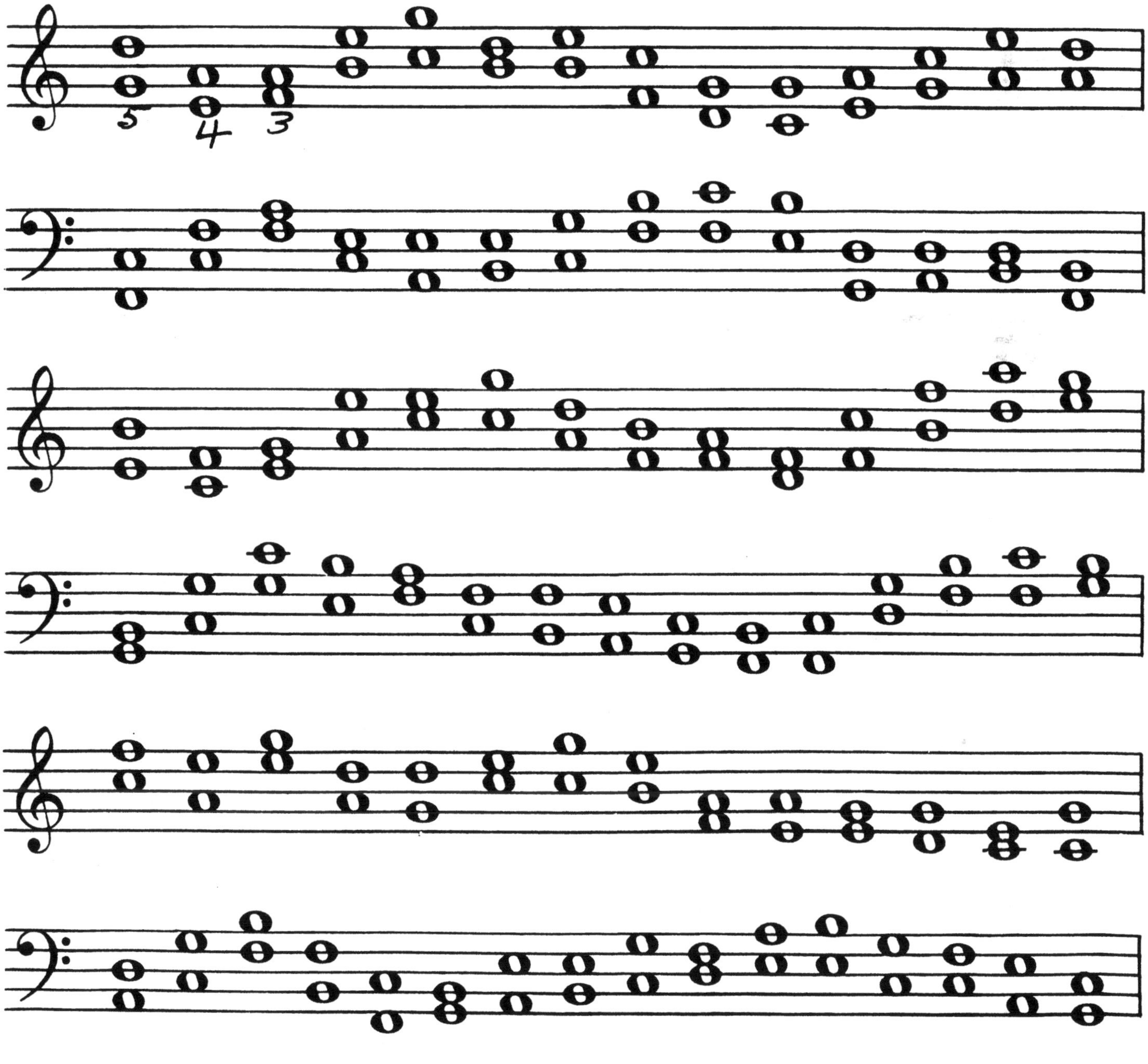

Draw the note a third, fourth, or fifth *above* each of these notes.
The number under each note will show you what kind of interval to draw.

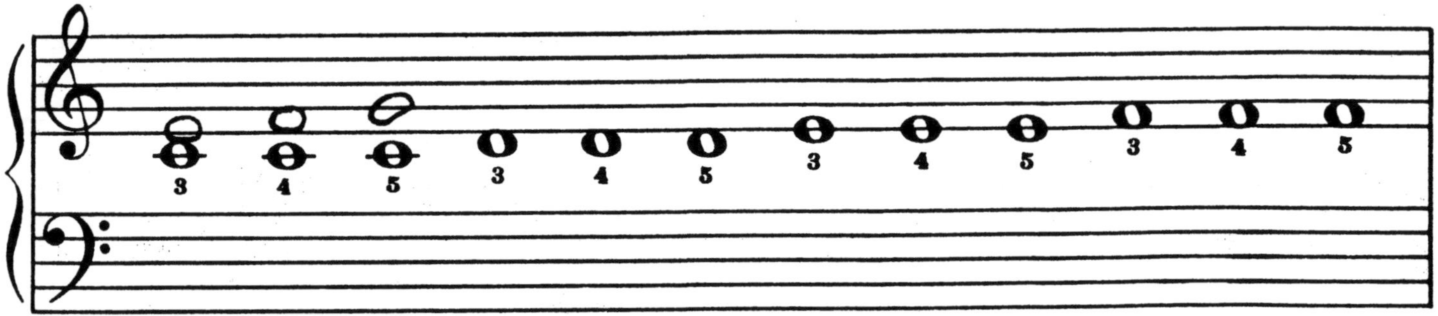

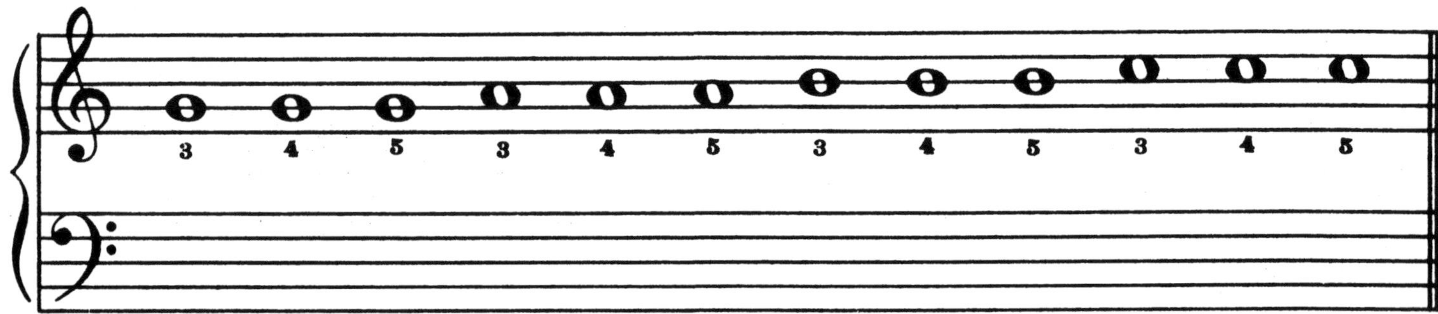

Draw the note a third, fourth, or fifth *below* each of these notes.
The number over each note will show you what kind of interval to draw.

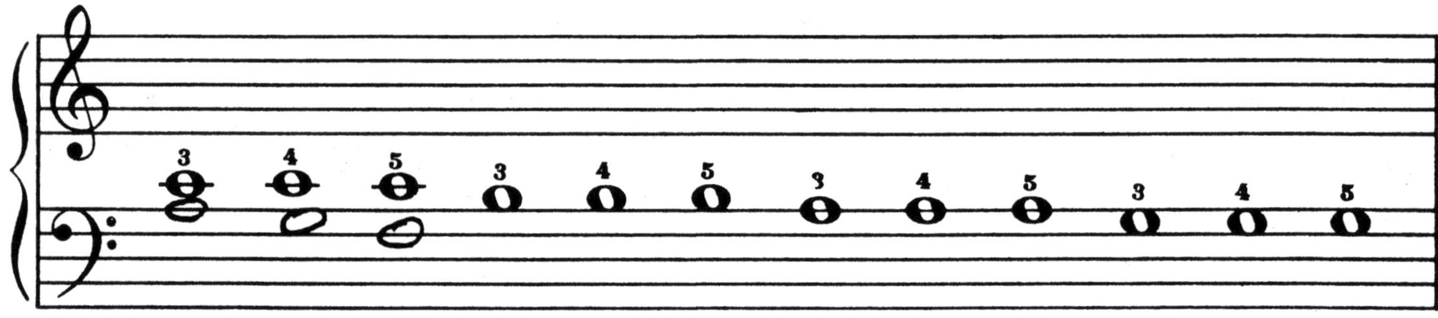

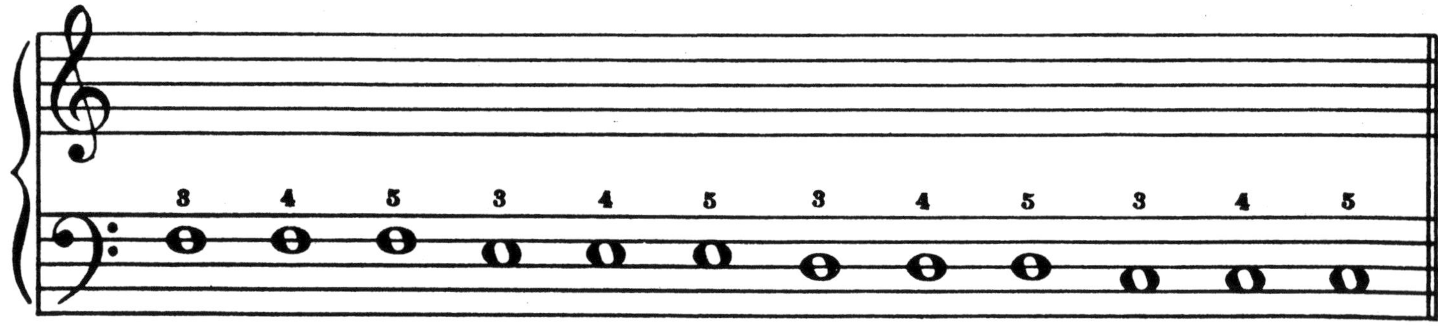

Play and recite the intervals on this page.

Draw the note a third, fourth, or fifth *above* each of these notes.
WATCH THE NUMBERS!

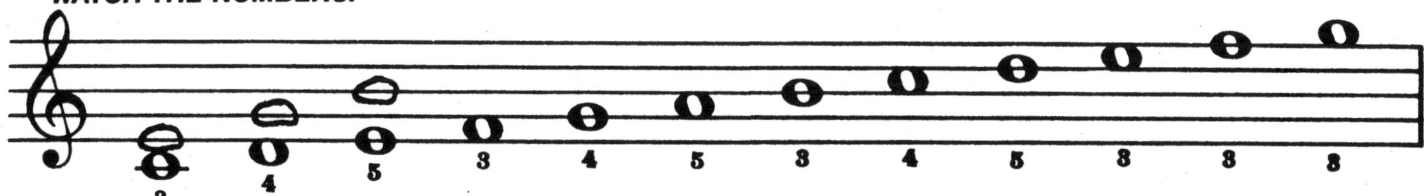

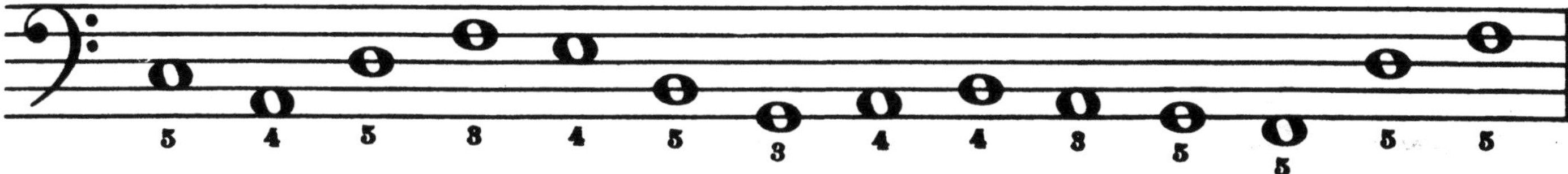

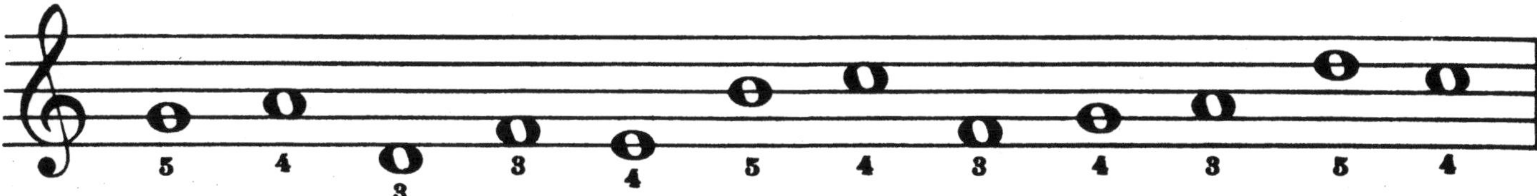

Draw the note a third, fourth, or fifth *below* each of these notes.
WATCH THE NUMBERS!

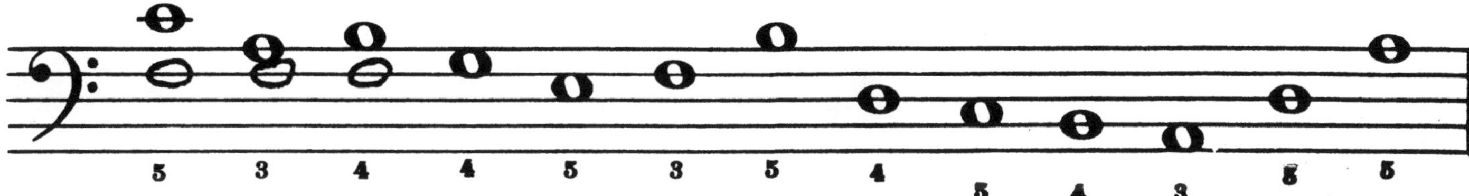

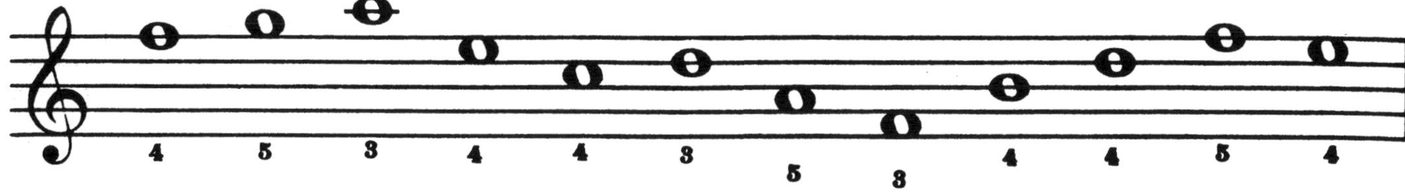

Dictation exercise:

Put the answer to each problem in its □

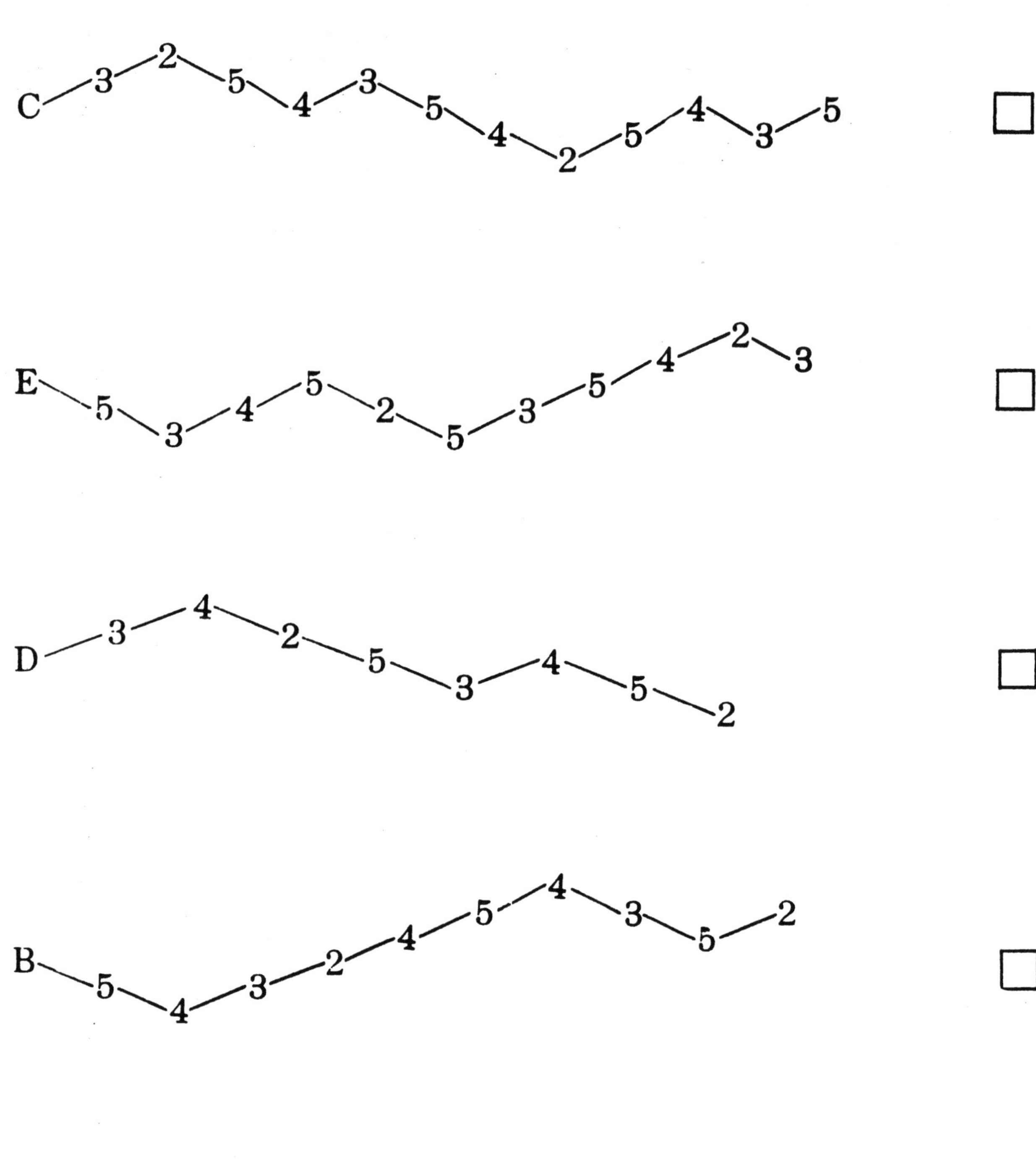

Starting with the note given, write the intervals indicated.

Up 3 5 4 2 Down 5 4 2 3 5 4

Up 4 4 3 5 5 4 Down 3 2 4 3 5

Up 3 3 2 5 4 Down 3 2 3 4 5

Up 3 4 2 3 3 Down 5 4 5 3 2 4

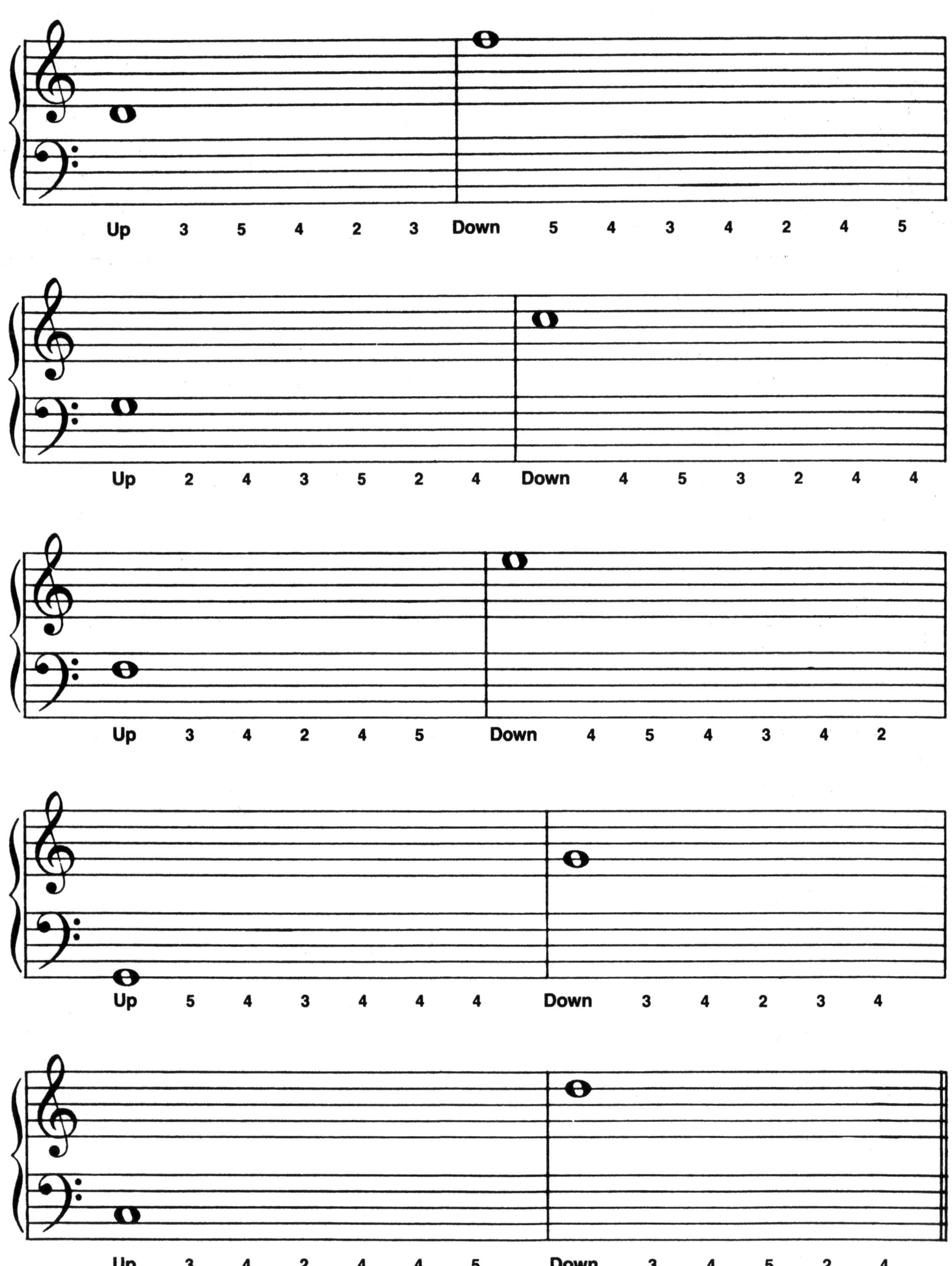

Now go back to the beginning and write the name under each of these notes.

Divide these notes into measures.

Complete each measure with *ONE* note. Use *ONE* note; not more than *ONE* note.

Swing and count each measure

More pieces for you to play – This time on thirds, fourths, and fifths.
DO NOT LOOK AT THE KEYBOARD!